# Big Data :

# The Beginner's Guide

By

Dr Bienvenue Ngoy

# Contents

# CHAPTER 1: HISTORY OF BIG DATA

The concept of "**big data**" can be traced back to the early days of computing, when the first electronic computers were used to process large amounts of data. However, the term "big data" did not become popular until the early 2000s, when it was used to describe the explosion of digital data that was being generated at an unprecedented rate.

In the 1990s, the development of the World Wide Web and the widespread adoption of the Internet led to an explosion of digital data. This data was being generated by a wide variety of sources, including social media, online transactions, and sensor networks.

As the amount of data being generated continued to grow, it became increasingly difficult to manage and analyze. In response, a new field of study emerged, known as "data science," which focused on developing new methods and tools for managing and analyzing large datasets.

One of the key developments in the history of big data was the emergence of Hadoop, an open-source software framework that allows for the distributed processing of large datasets. Hadoop was developed by Doug Cutting and Mike Cafarella in 2005, and it quickly became the standard tool for processing big data.

Another important development was the rise of cloud computing, which allowed organizations to store and process large amounts of data without having to invest in expensive hardware and infrastructure.

Today, big data is an essential part of many industries, including finance, healthcare, and marketing. It is used to analyze customer behavior, identify trends, and improve decision-making. As the amount of data being generated continues to grow, it is likely that the importance of big data will only continue to increase in the years to come.

## Questions and answers

Q: When did the concept of big data emerge? A: The concept of big data emerged in the early 2000s, as the volume and variety of data being generated began to increase exponentially.

Q: What were some of the key developments that led to the growth of big data? A: Some of the key developments that led to the growth of big data include the proliferation of the internet, the rise of social media and mobile devices, and the increasing digitization of business processes.

Q: What are some of the early examples of big data in use? A: Some early examples of big data in use include Google's search algorithms, Amazon's product recommendations, and Facebook's social network analysis.

Q: How has big data impacted business? A: Big data has had a significant impact on business, enabling organizations to gain insights into customer behavior, streamline operations, and make data-driven decisions.

Q: What are some of the challenges associated with big data? A: Some of the challenges associated with big data include managing the volume and variety of data, ensuring data quality and security, and developing the skills and infrastructure needed to analyze and interpret data.

Q: How has the technology for processing and analyzing big data evolved over time? A: The technology for processing and analyzing big data has evolved rapidly over time, with innovations such as Hadoop, NoSQL databases, and cloud computing enabling organizations to store, process, and analyze large volumes of data more efficiently and cost-effectively.

Q: What are some of the potential future developments in the field of big data? A: Some potential future developments in the field of big data include the increasing use of artificial intelligence and machine learning, the growth of the Internet of Things, and the emergence of new data privacy and security regulations.

# Career in big data

A career in big data can be very promising, as the field of big data continues to grow and evolve rapidly. Here are some potential career paths in big data:

1. **Data Analyst**: A data analyst is responsible for collecting, analyzing, and interpreting large sets of data to identify trends and insights that can be used to improve business decisions. They work with tools such as SQL, Excel, and Tableau to manipulate and visualize data.
2. **Data Scientist**: A data scientist uses advanced statistical and machine learning techniques to

identify patterns and insights in data. They develop and implement predictive models and algorithms to help businesses make informed decisions.

3. **Big Data Engineer**: A big data engineer is responsible for designing, building, and maintaining the infrastructure that supports large-scale data processing. They work with technologies such as Hadoop, Spark, and NoSQL databases to develop scalable and reliable systems.

4. **Business Intelligence Analyst**: A business intelligence analyst is responsible for using data to help businesses make informed decisions. They work with tools such as Power BI, QlikView, and SAP to create reports and dashboards that provide insights into business operations.

5. **Machine Learning Engineer**: A machine learning engineer is responsible for designing, building, and deploying machine learning models and algorithms. They work with technologies such as Python, TensorFlow, and Keras to develop and test models that can be integrated into business applications.

# Certifications in Big data

**There are several certifications** available in the field of big data that can help professionals demonstrate their skills and knowledge to potential employers. Here are some of the most popular certifications:

1. **Cloudera Certified Data Analyst**: This certification validates a professional's skills in analyzing data with Hive and Impala, as well as visualizing data using tools such as Tableau and Excel.

2. **IBM Certified Data Engineer - Big Data**: This certification validates a professional's skills in designing, building, and maintaining Big Data solutions using Hadoop, Spark, and NoSQL databases.

3. **Hortonworks Certified Associate (HCA):** This certification validates a professional's skills in using Hadoop and related technologies for data analysis and processing.

4. **Microsoft Certified**: Azure Data Scientist Associate: This certification validates a professional's skills in using Microsoft Azure

tools and technologies to design and implement machine learning solutions.

5. **SAS Certified Big Data Professional**: This certification validates a professional's skills in using SAS tools and technologies for data analysis and processing.

These certifications can help professionals stand out in a competitive job market and demonstrate their expertise to potential employers. It's important to note that certifications are not a substitute for real-world experience, but they can complement it and help professionals stay up-to-date with the latest tools and technologies in the field of big data.

# CHAPTER 2 : INTRODUCTION TO BIG DATA , TYPES, CHARACTERISTICS, EXAMPLES

**Big data** refers to extremely large, complex and diverse sets of data that require advanced tools and techniques to store, process, and analyze. This data can come from a wide range of sources, such as social media, sensors, weblogs, transactional data, and more. Big data is characterized by its high volume, velocity, and variety, often referred to as the "3 Vs" of big data.

The amount of data generated worldwide has been increasing at an exponential rate, and it is expected to reach 175 zettabytes by 2025. Big data has the potential to revolutionize many industries, including healthcare, finance, retail, and manufacturing. It can be used to identify patterns and insights, make more informed decisions, and improve business processes.

However, big data also poses significant challenges, such as data quality, privacy, and security concerns. The sheer volume of data can also make it difficult to manage and analyze. To address these challenges, specialized tools and techniques have been developed, such as Hadoop, Spark, and machine learning algorithms.

Overall, big data has become a critical component of modern business and technology, and its importance is only expected to grow in the coming years.
Big data analysis is the process of examining and interpreting large, complex data sets in order to uncover hidden patterns, correlations, and insights. This analysis can be used to help businesses make informed decisions, optimize operations, and identify new opportunities.

The process of big data analysis typically involves the following steps:

1. **Data collection**: The first step is to collect and aggregate large volumes of data from various sources. This data can come from structured, semi-structured, or unstructured sources.

2. **Data preprocessing**: Once the data is collected, it needs to be cleaned, transformed, and formatted to make it suitable for analysis. This may involve removing missing values, normalizing the data, or converting it to a different format.

3. **Data storage:** The preprocessed data is stored in a distributed file system like Hadoop Distributed File System (HDFS), which is designed to handle large volumes of data.

4. **Data analysis:** The next step is to apply various analytical techniques to the data to uncover patterns and insights. This may involve using statistical analysis, machine learning algorithms, or data visualization tools.

5. **Interpretation**: After the data has been analyzed, the results are interpreted to extract meaningful insights that can be used to make informed decisions.

Some common techniques used in big data analysis include data mining, predictive modeling, sentiment analysis, and anomaly detection. These techniques can be used to address a variety of business problems, such as customer segmentation, fraud detection, supply chain optimization, and risk management.

**Big data and the Internet of Things (IoT)** are two technologies that are closely related and often used together. The IoT refers to the network of physical devices, vehicles, appliances, and other items that are embedded with sensors, software, and connectivity, which allows them to collect and exchange data.

The data generated by IoT devices can be enormous, and big data technologies are often used to analyze and make sense of this data. By combining the data generated by various IoT devices, organizations can gain insights into customer behavior, supply chain operations, and more.

Some common use cases of big data and IoT include:

1. **Predictive maintenance**: By analyzing data from IoT sensors, organizations can detect and predict equipment failures before they

occur, allowing them to schedule maintenance and avoid costly downtime.

2. **Smart cities**: IoT sensors can be used to monitor traffic patterns, air quality, and other factors in urban areas, allowing city officials to make more informed decisions about infrastructure and resource allocation.

3. **Agriculture**: IoT sensors can be used to monitor soil moisture, crop growth, and other factors, allowing farmers to optimize their operations and improve yields.

4. **Healthcare**: IoT devices can be used to monitor patients' health remotely, allowing healthcare providers to provide more personalized care and detect potential health issues before they become serious.

# What is Data?

**Data** refers to any piece of information, fact, or statistics that can be stored, analyzed, and used to support decision-making. Data can take many forms, including numbers, text, images, audio, and video.

Data can be **structured** or **unstructured**. Structured data is organized in a specific format, such as a spreadsheet or database, making it easier to search, analyze, and manipulate. Unstructured data, on the other hand, does not have a specific format and can include text documents, social media posts, and images, among other things.

Data is collected from a wide variety of sources, such as sensors, social media platforms, surveys, and customer transactions. It is often processed and analyzed using specialized tools and techniques, such as machine learning algorithms and statistical analysis.

The insights gained from analyzing data can help organizations make more informed decisions, identify patterns and trends, and improve business processes. Data is a critical component of many industries, including finance, healthcare, marketing, and manufacturing, among others.

The quantities, characters, or symbols on which operations are performed by a computer, which may be stored and transmitted in the form of electrical signals and recorded on magnetic, optical, or mechanical recording media.

Now, let's learn Big Data definition

# What is Big Data?

**Big Data** is a collection of data that is huge in volume, yet growing exponentially with time. It is a data with so large size and complexity that none of traditional data management tools can store it or process it efficiently. Big data is also a data but with huge size.

In this Big Data analytics book, you will learn,

- What is Data?
- What is Big Data?
- What is an Example of Big Data?
- Types Of Big Data
- Characteristics Of Big Data
- Advantages Of Big Data Processing

# Example of Big Data

Following are some of the Big Data examples-

The **New York Stock Exchange** is an example of Big Data that generates about *one terabyte* of new trade data per day.

**Social Media**

The statistic shows that *500+terabytes* of new data get ingested into the databases of social media site **Facebook**, every day. This data is mainly generated in terms of photo and video uploads, message exchanges, putting comments etc.

A single **Jet engine** can generate *10+terabytes* of data in *30 minutes* of flight time. With many thousand flights per day, generation of data reaches up to many *Petabytes.*

There are many real-world scenarios where big data is used to gain insights and drive decision-making. Here are a few examples:

1. **Healthcare**: Big data is used in healthcare to analyze patient data, identify patterns, and improve outcomes. For example, healthcare organizations can use big data to monitor patients in real-time, identify those at high risk of developing certain conditions, and develop personalized treatment plans.

2. **Finance**: Big data is used in finance to analyze market trends, identify investment opportunities, and manage risk. Financial

institutions can use big data to monitor customer behavior, detect fraudulent transactions, and develop targeted marketing campaigns.

3. **Manufacturing**: Big data is used in manufacturing to optimize production processes, reduce downtime, and improve product quality. Manufacturers can use big data to monitor machines in real-time, detect potential issues before they occur, and optimize maintenance schedules.

4. **Transportation**: Big data is used in transportation to optimize routes, reduce congestion, and improve safety. Transportation companies can use big data to monitor traffic patterns, predict delays, and develop more efficient routing strategies.

5. **Retail**: Big data is used in retail to analyze customer behavior, optimize pricing strategies, and improve supply chain management. Retailers can use big data to monitor customer purchases, analyze social media data, and develop targeted marketing campaigns.

# Questions and answers

Q: What is big data? A: Big data refers to large and complex datasets that are difficult to process and analyze using traditional data processing tools.

Q: What are the three main characteristics of big data? A: The three main characteristics of big data are volume (the sheer amount of data), velocity (the speed at which data is generated and processed), and variety (the different types and sources of data).

Q: What are the three types of big data? A: The three types of big data are structured data, unstructured data, and semi-structured data.

Q: What is structured data? A: Structured data refers to data that is organized in a specific format, such as rows and columns in a database or spreadsheet.

Q: What is unstructured data? A: Unstructured data refers to data that is not organized in a specific format, such as text documents, images, and videos.

Q: What is semi-structured data? A: Semi-structured data refers to data that has some organizational structure but does not fit neatly into a traditional structured format, such as XML files or social media data.

Q: What are some examples of big data in use? A: Some examples of big data in use include personalized advertising based on user behavior, real-time traffic monitoring, and predictive maintenance in manufacturing.

Q: How has big data impacted businesses? A: Big data has had a significant impact on businesses, enabling them to gain insights into customer behavior, streamline operations, and make data-driven decisions.

Q: What are some of the challenges associated with big data? A: Some of the challenges associated with big data include managing the volume and variety of data, ensuring data quality and security, and developing the skills and infrastructure needed to analyze and interpret data.

Q: What are some of the technologies used for processing and analyzing big data? A: Some of the technologies used for processing and analyzing big data include Hadoop, NoSQL databases, and cloud computing.

Q: What are some potential future developments in the field of big data? A: Some potential future developments in the field of big data include the increasing use of artificial intelligence and machine learning, the growth of the Internet of Things, and the emergence of new data privacy and security regulations.

# CHAPTER 3 : TYPES OF BIG DATA

Following are the types of Big Data:

1. **Structured**
2. **Unstructured**
3. **Semi-structured**

## Structured

Any data that can be stored, accessed and processed in the form of fixed format is termed as a 'structured' data. Over the period of time, talent in computer science has achieved greater success in developing techniques for working with such kind of data (where the format is well known in advance) and also deriving value out of it. However, nowadays, we are foreseeing issues when a size of such data grows to a huge extent, typical sizes are being in the rage of multiple zettabytes.

**Structured data**: This type of data is organized and follows a specific format, making it easy to store, process, and analyze. Structured data is typically stored in databases or spreadsheets and can include things like transactional data, sensor data, and customer data.

---

*Do you know? $10^{21}$ bytes* equal to *1 zettabyte* or *one billion terabytes* forms *a zettabyte*.

---

Looking at these figures one can easily understand why the name Big Data is given and imagine the challenges involved in its storage and processing.

---

*Do you know?* Data stored in a relational database management system is one example of a **'structured'** data.

---

**Examples Of Structured Data**

An 'Employee' table in a database is an example of Structured Data

| Employee_ID | Employee_Name | Gender | Department | Salary_In_lacs |
|---|---|---|---|---|
| 2365 | Rajesh Kulkarni | Male | Finance | 650000 |
| 3398 | Pratibha Joshi | Female | Admin | 650000 |
| 7465 | Shushil Roy | Male | Admin | 500000 |
| 7500 | Shubhojit Das | Male | Finance | 500000 |
| 7699 | Priya Sane | Female | Finance | 550000 |

Structured data is organized and follows a specific format, making it easy to store, process, and analyze. Here are some examples of structured data:

1. **Sales data**: This can include information such as the date of the sale, the product sold, the price, and the customer information.
2. **Customer data**: This can include information such as name, address, phone number, and email address.
3. **Financial data**: This can include data related to financial transactions, such as credit card transactions, bank transfers, and stock trades.
4. **Inventory data**: This can include information on the quantity, location, and status of inventory items.
5. **Employee data**: This can include information such as employee names, addresses, contact details, job titles, and salaries.
6. **Weblog data**: This can include information on website visitors, such as their IP address,

the pages they visited, and the time they spent on each page.

7. **Healthcare data**: This can include patient data, such as medical history, diagnoses, and treatments.

# Unstructured

Any data with unknown form or the structure is classified as unstructured data. In addition to the size being huge, un-structured data poses multiple challenges in terms of its processing for deriving value out of it. A typical example of unstructured data is a heterogeneous data source containing a combination of simple text files, images, videos etc. Now day organizations have wealth of data available with them but unfortunately, they don't know how to derive value out of it since this data is in its raw form or unstructured format.

**Examples Of Un-structured Data**

The output returned by 'Google Search'

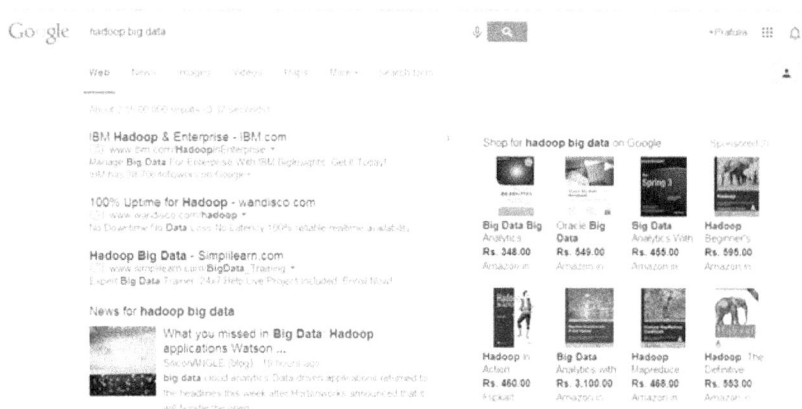

## Example Of Un-structured Data

Unstructured data does not have a specific format and can take many different forms. Here are some examples of unstructured data:

1. **Text data**: This can include email messages, social media posts, news articles, and chat logs.
2. **Image data**: This can include photographs, videos, and scanned documents.
3. **Audio data**: This can include voice recordings, music files, and podcasts.
4. **Social media data**: This can include data from social media platforms such as Twitter, Facebook, and Instagram, including posts, comments, and likes.

5. **Web page data**: This can include HTML, CSS, and JavaScript code that makes up web pages.
6. **Sensor data**: This can include data from sensors and other IoT devices, such as temperature sensors, GPS trackers, and smart meters.
7. **Customer feedback data**: This can include feedback from customer surveys, product reviews, and customer support chats.

## Semi-structured

Semi-structured data can contain both the forms of data. We can see semi-structured data as a structured in form but it is actually not defined with e.g. a table definition in relational DBMS. Example of semi-structured data is a data represented in an XML file.

Examples Of Semi-structured Data

Personal data stored in an XML file-

```
<rec><name>Prashant
Rao</name><sex>Male</sex><age>35</age></rec>
<rec><name>Seema
R.</name><sex>Female</sex><age>41</age></rec>
<rec><name>Satish
Mane</name><sex>Male</sex><age>29</age></rec>
```

```
<rec><name>Subrato
Roy</name><sex>Male</sex><age>26</age></rec>
<rec><name>Jeremiah
J.</name><sex>Male</sex><age>35</age></rec>
```

## Data Growth over the years

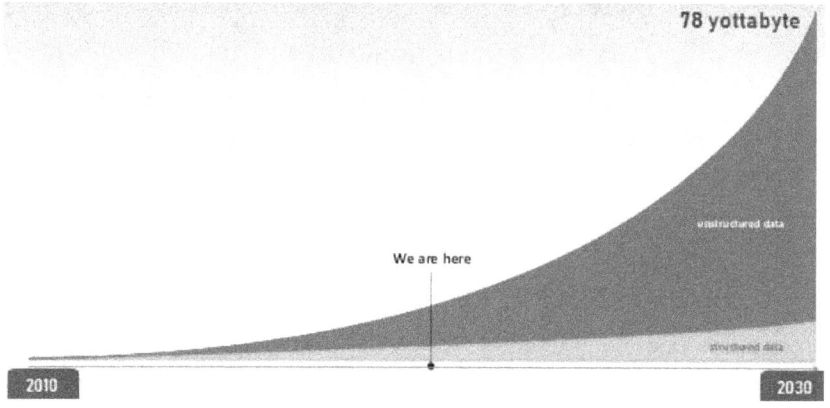

Data Growth over the years

Please note that web application data, which is unstructured, consists of log files, transaction history files etc. OLTP systems are built to work with structured data wherein data is stored in relations (tables).

Semi-structured data has some structure, but it is not as rigid as structured data. Here are some examples of semi-structured data:

1. **XML data**: This is a markup language used to encode documents that can include nested elements, attributes, and values.
2. **JSON data**: This is a lightweight data interchange format that is easy for humans to read and write, and easy for machines to parse and generate.
3. **Log files**: This can include server logs, system logs, and application logs, which can contain valuable information on errors, warnings, and system performance.
4. **Email data**: This can include email headers, attachments, and metadata.
5. **NoSQL databases**: This is a type of database that is designed to handle semi-structured and unstructured data.
6. **Web data**: This can include web page metadata, such as titles, descriptions, and keywords.
7. **Sensor data**: This can include data from sensors and other IoT devices that have some structure, such as GPS coordinates and time stamps.

Questions and answers

Q: What are the three main types of big data?
A: The three main types of big data are
structured data, unstructured data, and semi-
structured data.

Q: What is structured data? A: Structured data
refers to data that is organized in a specific
format, such as rows and columns in a
database or spreadsheet.

Q: What are some examples of structured
data? A: Examples of structured data include
customer data, transaction data, and inventory
data.

Q: What is unstructured data? A: Unstructured
data refers to data that is not organized in a
specific format, such as text documents,
images, and videos.

Q: What are some examples of unstructured
data? A: Examples of unstructured data
include social media posts, emails, and
surveillance footage.

Q: What is semi-structured data? A: Semi-
structured data refers to data that has some
organizational structure but does not fit neatly

into a traditional structured format, such as XML files or social media data.

Q: What are some examples of semi-structured data? A: Examples of semi-structured data include log files, sensor data, and metadata.

Q: How is structured data typically stored? A: Structured data is typically stored in relational databases or spreadsheets.

Q: How is unstructured data typically stored? A: Unstructured data is typically stored in file systems or NoSQL databases.

Q: How is semi-structured data typically stored? A: Semi-structured data is typically stored in XML files or NoSQL databases.

Q: What are some of the challenges associated with processing and analyzing each type of big data? A: Processing and analyzing structured data can be challenging due to its size and complexity, while unstructured data presents challenges related to its lack of structure and difficulty in identifying meaningful insights. Semi-structured data can be challenging due to its varying levels of structure and complexity.

# CHAPTER 4 : CHARACTERISTICS OF BIG DATA

Big data can be described by the following characteristics:

> Volume
> Variety
> Velocity
> Variability

*(i) Volume* – The name Big Data itself is related to a size which is enormous. Size of data plays a very crucial role in determining value out of data. Also, whether a particular data can actually be considered as a Big Data or not, is dependent upon the volume of data. Hence, **'Volume'** is one characteristic which needs to be considered while dealing with Big Data solutions.

*(ii) Variety* – The next aspect of Big Data is its **variety**.

Variety refers to heterogeneous sources and the nature of data, both structured and unstructured. During earlier days, spreadsheets and databases were the only sources of data considered by most of the applications. Nowadays, data in the form of emails, photos, videos, monitoring devices, PDFs, audio, etc. are also being considered in the analysis applications. This variety of unstructured data poses certain issues for storage, mining and analyzing data.

*(iii) Velocity* – The term **'velocity'** refers to the speed of generation of data. How fast the data is generated and processed to meet the demands, determines real potential in the data.

Big Data Velocity deals with the speed at which data flows in from sources like business processes, application logs, networks, and social media sites, sensors, Mobile devices, etc. The flow of data is massive and continuous.

*(iv) Variability* – This refers to the inconsistency which can be shown by the data at times, thus hampering the process of being able to handle and manage the data effectively.

# Advantages Of Big Data Processing

Big data processing offers several advantages for organizations that need to store, process, and analyze large amounts of data. Here are some of the key advantages of big data processing:

1. **Better decision-making**: Big data processing can help organizations make more informed decisions by providing valuable insights into customer behavior, market trends, and business performance.
2. **Improved efficiency**: By automating data processing tasks, big data processing can help organizations save time and reduce costs.
3. **Competitive advantage**: Big data processing can help organizations gain a competitive advantage by identifying new opportunities, improving product development, and enhancing customer experiences.
4. **Personalized experiences**: By analyzing customer data, big data processing can help organizations personalize their products and services to better meet the needs of individual customers.
5. **Predictive analytics**: Big data processing can enable organizations to use predictive analytics to forecast trends and anticipate customer needs, improving their ability to plan and strategize for the future.

6. **Scalability**: Big data processing technologies are highly scalable, allowing organizations to store and process ever-increasing amounts of data as their needs grow.

Ability to process Big Data in DBMS brings in multiple benefits, such as-

- **Businesses can utilize outside intelligence while taking decisions**

Access to social data from search engines and sites like facebook, twitter are enabling organizations to fine tune their business strategies.

- **Improved customer service**

Traditional customer feedback systems are getting replaced by new systems designed with Big Data technologies. In these new systems, Big Data and natural language processing technologies are being used to read and evaluate consumer responses.

➢ Early identification of risk to the product/services, if any
➢ Better operational efficiency

Big Data technologies can be used for creating a staging area or landing zone for new data before identifying what data should be moved to the data warehouse. In addition, such integration of Big Data technologies and data warehouse helps an organization to offload infrequently accessed data.

# Summary

- Big Data definition : Big Data meaning a data that is huge in size. Bigdata is a term used to describe a collection of data that is huge in size and yet growing exponentially with time.
- Big Data analytics examples includes stock exchanges, social media sites, jet engines, etc.
- Big Data could be 1) Structured, 2) Unstructured, 3) Semi-structured
- Volume, Variety, Velocity, and Variability are few Big Data characteristics
- Improved customer service, better operational efficiency, Better Decision Making are few advantages of Bigdata

## Questions and answers

Q: What are the main characteristics of big data? A: The main characteristics of big data are volume, velocity, and variety.

Q: What is volume in the context of big data? A: Volume refers to the vast amounts of data that are generated and collected every day.

Q: What is velocity in the context of big data? A: Velocity refers to the speed at which data is generated and processed.

Q: What is variety in the context of big data? A: Variety refers to the different types and sources of data that are generated and collected, including structured, unstructured, and semi-structured data.

Q: What are some examples of high volume data? A: Examples of high volume data include social media posts, IoT sensor data, and financial transactions.

Q: What are some examples of high velocity data? A: Examples of high velocity data include stock market data, real-time traffic updates, and online gaming data.

Q: What are some examples of high variety data? A: Examples of high variety data include multimedia content such as images, audio, and video, as well as text data such as emails, social media posts, and web content.

Q: What are some challenges associated with big data volume? A: Challenges associated with big data volume include the need for scalable storage and processing solutions, as well as challenges related to data quality and integrity.

Q: What are some challenges associated with big data velocity? A: Challenges associated with big data velocity include the need for real-time or near-real-time processing capabilities, as well as challenges related to data latency and reliability.

Q: What are some challenges associated with big data variety? A: Challenges associated with big data variety include the need for data integration and cleansing solutions, as well as challenges related to data governance and compliance.

# CHAPTER 5 : HADOOP:  INTRODUCTION, ARCHITECTURE, ECOSYSTEM, COMPONENTS

## What is Hadoop?

Apache Hadoop is an open source software framework used to develop data processing applications which are executed in a distributed computing environment.

Applications built using **HADOOP** are run on large data sets distributed across clusters of commodity computers. Commodity computers are cheap and widely available. These are mainly useful for achieving greater computational power at low cost.

**Hadoop** is an open-source distributed computing platform that enables the processing and storage of large datasets across clusters of computers. The platform is designed to be scalable, fault-tolerant, and cost-effective, making it a popular choice for big data processing.

Hadoop consists of two main components:

1. **Hadoop Distributed File System (HDFS):** This is a distributed file system that provides a way to store and manage large datasets across multiple machines. HDFS is designed to be fault-tolerant, meaning that it can continue to operate even if some of the nodes in the cluster fail.
2. **MapReduce**: This is a programming model and software framework for processing large

datasets in parallel across multiple nodes in a Hadoop cluster. MapReduce divides the data into smaller chunks and distributes them across the cluster, allowing the processing to be done in parallel.

Hadoop is widely used in industries such as finance, healthcare, and telecommunications for processing large datasets. It is particularly useful for applications such as log processing, data warehousing, and machine learning.

Some of the benefits of Hadoop include:

1. **Scalability**: Hadoop can scale up to handle very large datasets by adding more nodes to the cluster.
2. **Cost-effectiveness**: Hadoop is designed to run on commodity hardware, making it more cost-effective than traditional enterprise storage solutions.
3. **Fault tolerance**: Hadoop's distributed architecture provides built-in fault tolerance, making it more resilient to node failures.
4. **Flexibility**: Hadoop is compatible with a wide range of data formats and can be used with a variety of programming languages.

Similar to data residing in a local file system of a personal computer system, in Hadoop, data resides in a distributed file system which is called as a **Hadoop Distributed File system**. The processing model is based on **'Data Locality'** concept wherein computational logic is sent to cluster nodes(server) containing data. This computational logic is nothing, but a compiled version of a program written in a high-level language such as Java. Such a program, processes data stored in Hadoop HDFS.

*Do you know?* Computer cluster consists of a set of multiple processing units (storage disk + processor) which are connected to each other and acts as a single system.

In this book, you will learn,

- Hadoop EcoSystem and Components
- Hadoop Architecture
- Features Of 'Hadoop'
- Network Topology In Hadoop

# Hadoop EcoSystem and Components

Below diagram shows various components in the Hadoop ecosystem-

Apache Hadoop consists of two sub-projects –

1. **Hadoop MapReduce:** MapReduce is a computational model and software framework for writing applications which are run on Hadoop. These MapReduce programs are capable of processing enormous data in parallel on large clusters of computation nodes.

2. **HDFS (Hadoop Distributed File System):** HDFS takes care of the storage part of Hadoop applications. MapReduce applications consume data from HDFS. HDFS creates multiple replicas of data blocks and distributes

them on compute nodes in a cluster. This distribution enables reliable and extremely rapid computations.

Although Hadoop is best known for MapReduce and its distributed file system- HDFS, the term is also used for a family of related projects that fall under the umbrella of distributed computing and large-scale data processing. Other Hadoop-related projects at Apache include are **Hive, HBase, Mahout, Sqoop, Flume, and ZooKeeper.**

# Hadoop Architecture

The Hadoop architecture is designed to enable the processing and storage of large datasets across a cluster of commodity hardware. It consists of several components that work together to provide a distributed computing platform for big data processing. Here is an overview of the key components of the Hadoop architecture:

1. **Hadoop Distributed File System (HDFS):** HDFS is a distributed file system that stores large datasets across multiple machines in a Hadoop cluster. HDFS provides fault

tolerance and high availability by replicating data across multiple nodes in the cluster.

2. **NameNode**: The NameNode is the central component of HDFS and is responsible for managing the file system metadata. It keeps track of the location of data blocks and manages the replication of data across the cluster.

3. **DataNode**: DataNodes are the nodes in the HDFS cluster that store the actual data. Each DataNode stores a subset of the data and communicates with the NameNode to manage data replication and retrieval.

4. **MapReduce**: MapReduce is a programming model and software framework for processing large datasets in parallel across multiple nodes in a Hadoop cluster. MapReduce divides the data into smaller chunks and distributes them across the cluster, allowing the processing to be done in parallel.

5. **YARN** (Yet Another Resource Negotiator): YARN is the resource management system for Hadoop that manages resources such as memory and CPU across the cluster. It enables different processing engines, such as MapReduce and Apache Spark, to run on the same Hadoop cluster.

6. **JobTracker**: The JobTracker is the central component of the MapReduce framework and is responsible for scheduling and managing jobs across the cluster. It communicates with the TaskTrackers on each node in the cluster to assign tasks and monitor their progress.

7. **TaskTracker**: TaskTrackers are the nodes in the MapReduce cluster that run the actual processing tasks. They receive tasks from the JobTracker and communicate their progress back to the JobTracker.

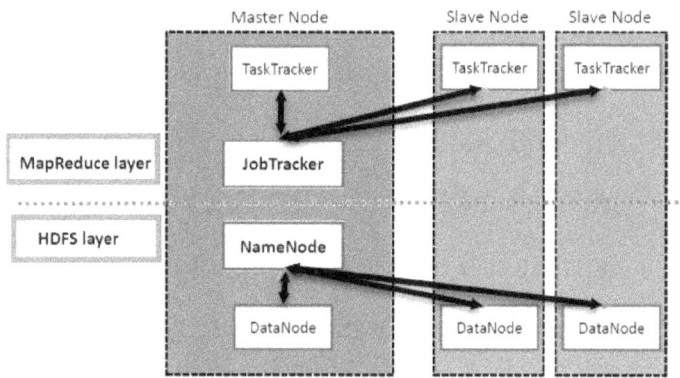

High Level Hadoop Architecture

Hadoop has a Master-Slave Architecture for data storage and distributed data processing using MapReduce and HDFS methods.

**NameNode:**

NameNode represented every files and directory which is used in the namespace

**DataNode:**

DataNode helps you to manage the state of an HDFS node and allows you to interacts with the blocks

**MasterNode:**

The master node allows you to conduct parallel processing of data using Hadoop MapReduce.

**Slave node:**

The slave nodes are the additional machines in the Hadoop cluster which allows you to store data to conduct complex calculations. Moreover, all the slave node comes with Task Tracker and a DataNode. This allows you to synchronize the processes with the NameNode and Job Tracker respectively.

In Hadoop, master or slave system can be set up in the cloud or on-premise

# Features Of 'Hadoop'

• **Suitable for Big Data Analysis**

As Big Data tends to be distributed and unstructured in nature, HADOOP clusters are best suited for analysis of Big Data. Since it is processing logic (not the actual data) that flows to the computing nodes, less network bandwidth is consumed. This concept is called as **data locality concept** which helps increase the efficiency of Hadoop based applications.

• **Scalability**

HADOOP clusters can easily be scaled to any extent by adding additional cluster nodes and thus allows for the growth of Big Data. Also, scaling does not require modifications to application logic.

**• Fault Tolerance**

HADOOP ecosystem has a provision to replicate the input data on to other cluster nodes. That way, in the event of a cluster node failure, data processing can still proceed by using data stored on another cluster node.

# Network Topology In Hadoop

Topology (Arrangment) of the network, affects the performance of the Hadoop cluster when the size of the Hadoop cluster grows. In addition to the performance, one also needs to care about the high availability and handling of failures. In order to achieve this Hadoop, cluster formation makes use of network topology.

Typically, network bandwidth is an important factor to consider while forming any network. However, as measuring bandwidth could be difficult, in Hadoop, a network is represented as a tree and distance between nodes of this tree (number of hops) is considered as an important factor in the formation of Hadoop cluster. Here, the distance between two nodes is equal to sum of their distance to their closest common ancestor.

Hadoop cluster consists of a data center, the rack and the node which actually executes jobs. Here, data center consists of racks and rack consists of nodes. Network bandwidth available to processes varies depending upon the location of the processes. That is, the bandwidth available becomes lesser as we go away from-

- Processes on the same node
- Different nodes on the same rack
- Nodes on different racks of the same data center
- Nodes in different data centers

## Questions and answers

Q: What is Hadoop? A: Hadoop is an open-source software framework used for distributed storage and processing of large data sets.

Q: What is the main purpose of Hadoop? A: The main purpose of Hadoop is to provide a scalable and fault-tolerant platform for processing and analyzing big data.

Q: What is the Hadoop Distributed File System (HDFS)? A: HDFS is a distributed file system that provides reliable and scalable storage for large data sets across multiple machines.

Q: What is MapReduce in Hadoop? A: MapReduce is a programming model and processing framework used for distributed processing of large data sets across a Hadoop cluster.

Q: What is the Hadoop ecosystem? A: The Hadoop ecosystem refers to the various tools and technologies that have been developed around the Hadoop platform to extend its functionality and make it easier to use.

Q: What are some common components of the Hadoop ecosystem? A: Common components of the Hadoop ecosystem include Apache Hive, Apache Pig, Apache Spark, Apache HBase, and Apache Kafka.

Q: What is Apache Hive? A: Apache Hive is a data warehousing tool used for querying and analyzing data stored in Hadoop.

Q: What is Apache Pig? A: Apache Pig is a high-level platform for creating MapReduce programs used for analyzing large data sets.

Q: What is Apache Spark? A: Apache Spark is a fast and general-purpose data processing engine used for distributed processing of large data sets.

Q: What is Apache HBase? A: Apache HBase is a distributed, scalable, and column-oriented database built on top of Hadoop.

Q: What is Apache Kafka? A: Apache Kafka is a distributed streaming platform used for building real-time streaming data pipelines and applications.

Q: What are the benefits of using Hadoop for big data processing? A: Benefits of using Hadoop for big data processing include scalability, fault-tolerance, cost-effectiveness, and the ability to process various types of data.

## How to Install Hadoop with Step by Step Configuration on Linux Ubuntu

In this book, we will take you through step by step process to install Apache Hadoop on a Linux box (Ubuntu). This is 2 part process

- Part 1) Download and Install Hadoop
- Part 2) Configure Hadoop

There are 2 **Prerequisites**

- You must have Ubuntu installed and running
- You must have Java Installed.

# Part 1) Download and Install Hadoop

1. First, download the latest stable release of Hadoop from the Apache website. You can download it using the following command:

This will download Hadoop version 3.3.1. You can replace the version number in the URL with the latest version available.

2. Once the download is complete, extract the archive file using the following command:

3. Move the extracted directory to a location of your choice, such as `/usr/local/`:

4. Next, add the Hadoop binaries to your PATH environment variable by editing the `~/.bashrc` file:

```bash
nano ~/.bashrc
```

Add the following line at the end of the file:

```ruby
export PATH=$PATH:/usr/local/hadoop-3.3.1/bin
```

Save the file and exit the editor.

5. Reload the `~/.bashrc` file to update the environment variable:

```bash
source ~/.bashrc
```

6. Hadoop requires Java to be installed on your system. You can check if Java is already installed by running the following command:

```
java -version
```

If Java is not installed, you can install it using the following command:

```arduino
sudo apt-get install default-jdk
```

7. Finally, you can start using Hadoop by configuring it and running various Hadoop commands.

Note: These are general steps for installing Hadoop on Ubuntu. The specific steps may vary depending on the version of Hadoop you are installing and your specific environment. Please refer to the Hadoop documentation for more detailed instructions.

**Step 1)** Add a Hadoop system user using below command

```
sudo addgroup hadoop_
```

```
guru99@guru99-VirtualBox:~$ sudo addgroup hadoop_
[sudo] password for guru99:
Adding group `hadoop_' (GID 1001) ...
Done.
```

```
sudo adduser --ingroup hadoop_ hduser_
```

```
guru99@guru99-VirtualBox:~$ sudo adduser --ingroup hadoop_ hduser_
Adding user `hduser_' ...
Adding new user `hduser_' (1001) with group `hadoop_' ...
Creating home directory `/home/hduser_' ...
Copying files from `/etc/skel' ...
Enter new UNIX password:
Retype new UNIX password:
passwd: password updated successfully
Changing the user information for hduser_
Enter the new value, or press ENTER for the default
        Full Name []: Team
        Room Number []: 1
        Work Phone []: 1
        Home Phone []: 1
        Other []: 1
Is the information correct? [Y/n] y
guru99@guru99-VirtualBox:~$
```

Enter &
Remember
Password

Enter your password, name and other details.

**NOTE:** There is a possibility of below-mentioned error in this setup and installation process.

## "hduser is not in the sudoers file. This incident will be reported."

```
hduser_@ajayanand-Virtual-Ubuntu:/usr/local/newhadoop$ sudo mv hadoop-1.0.3 hado
op
[sudo] password for hduser_:
hduser_ is not in the sudoers file.  This incident will be reported.
hduser_@ajayanand-Virtual-Ubuntu:/usr/local/newhadoop$
```

This error can be resolved by Login as a root user

```
hduser_@guru99-VirtualBox:/$ su guru99
Password:
guru99@guru99-VirtualBox:/$
```
Guru99 is
Root user

Execute the command

```
sudo adduser hduser_ sudo
```

```
guru99@guru99-VirtualBox:~$ sudo adduser hduser_ sudo
Adding user `hduser_' to group `sudo' ...
Adding user hduser_ to group sudo
Done.
```

```
Re-login as hduser_
```

```
guru99@guru99-VirtualBox:/$ su hduser_
Password:
hduser_@guru99-VirtualBox:/$
```

**Step 2)** Configure SSH

In order to manage nodes in a cluster, Hadoop requires SSH access

First, switch user, enter the following command

```
su - hduser_
```

```
guru99@guru99-VirtualBox:~$ su - hduser_
Password:
hduser_@guru99-VirtualBox:~$
```

This command will create a new key.

```
ssh-keygen -t rsa -P ""
```

```
guru99@guru99-VirtualBox:~$ su - hduser_
Password:
hduser_@guru99-VirtualBox:~$ ssh-keygen -t rsa -P ""
Generating public/private rsa key pair.
Enter file in which to save the key (/home/hduser_/.ssh/id_rsa):
Created directory '/home/hduser_/.ssh'.
Your identification has been saved in /home/hduser_/.ssh/id_rsa.
Your public key has been saved in /home/hduser_/.ssh/id_rsa.pub.
The key fingerprint is:
07:e2:3f:7d:7d:d1:0d:9d:12:0e:e7:27:ab:47:4a:22 hduser_@guru99-VirtualBox
The key's randomart image is:
+--[ RSA 2048]----+
|            . o  |
|           = ...|
|        .  =.o.|
|       . .    =.o|
|      .ES... o .o|
|      ..oo +.  .|
|       o .o...  .|
|         . ..  . |
|                 |
+-----------------+
hduser_@guru99-VirtualBox:~$
```

Press Enter

Enable SSH access to local machine using this key.

```
cat $HOME/.ssh/id_rsa.pub >>
$HOME/.ssh/authorized_keys
```

```
hduser_@guru99-VirtualBox:~$
hduser_@guru99-VirtualBox:~$ cat $HOME/.ssh/id_rsa.pub >> $HOME/.ssh/authorized_keys
```

Now test SSH setup by connecting to localhost as 'hduser' user.

```
ssh localhost
```

```
hduser_@guru99-VirtualBox:/$ ssh localhost
The authenticity of host 'localhost (127.0.0.1)' can't be established.
ECDSA key fingerprint is 4a:78:f7:93:32:0a:c1:b4:24:e2:a6:78:d7:cb:20:d6.
Are you sure you want to continue connecting (yes/no)? yes
Warning: Permanently added 'localhost' (ECDSA) to the list of known hosts
Welcome to Ubuntu 12.04.1 LTS (GNU/Linux 3.2.0-29-generic-pae i686)

 * Documentation:  https://help.ubuntu.com/


The programs included with the Ubuntu system are free software;
the exact distribution terms for each program are described in the
individual files in /usr/share/doc/*/copyright.

Ubuntu comes with ABSOLUTELY NO WARRANTY, to the extent permitted by
applicable law.

hduser_@guru99-VirtualBox:~$
```

**Note:** Please note, if you see below error in response to 'ssh localhost', then there is a possibility that SSH is not available on this system-

```
hduser@guru99: ~
hduser@guru99:~$ ssh localhost
ssh: connect to host localhost port 22: Connection refused
hduser@guru99:~$
```

## To resolve this –

Purge SSH using,

```
sudo apt-get purge openssh-server
```
It is good practice to purge before the start of installation

```
hduser@guru99:~$ sudo apt-get purge openssh-server
Reading package lists... Done
Building dependency tree
Reading state information... Done
Package 'openssh-server' is not installed, so not removed
0 upgraded, 0 newly installed, 0 to remove and 19 not upgraded.
hduser@guru99:~$
```

Install SSH using the command-

```
sudo apt-get install openssh-server
```

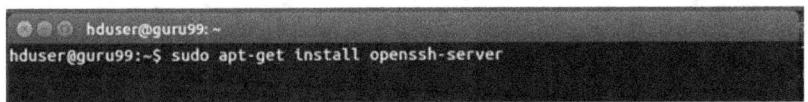

## Step 3) Next step is to Download Hadoop

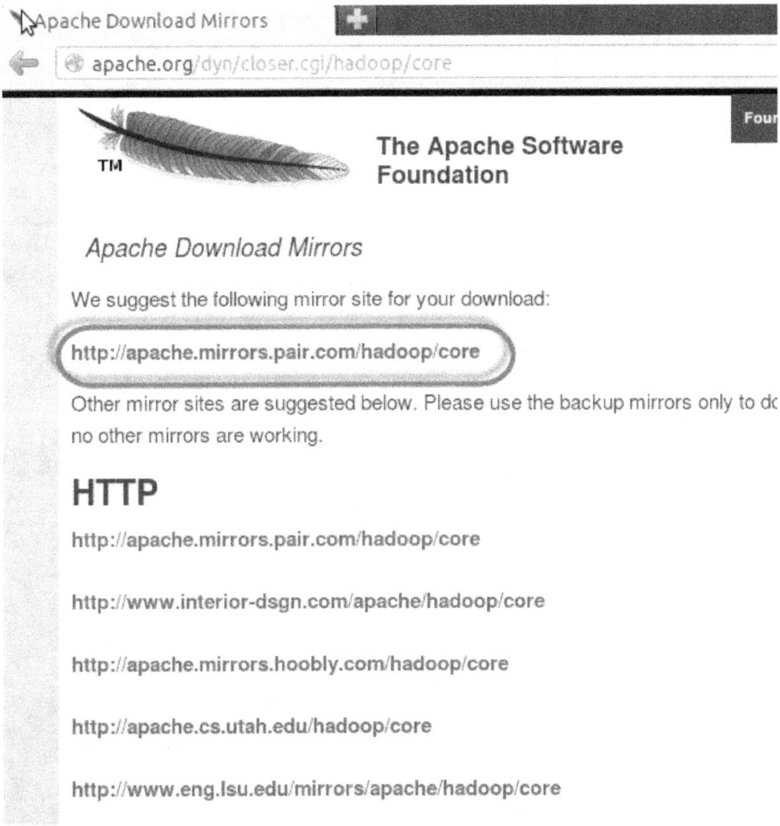

apache.org/dyn/closer.cgi/hadoop/core

**The Apache Software Foundation**

TM

*Apache Download Mirrors*

We suggest the following mirror site for your download:

http://apache.mirrors.pair.com/hadoop/core

Other mirror sites are suggested below. Please use the backup mirrors only to do
no other mirrors are working.

## HTTP

http://apache.mirrors.pair.com/hadoop/core

http://www.interior-dsgn.com/apache/hadoop/core

http://apache.mirrors.hoobly.com/hadoop/core

http://apache.cs.utah.edu/hadoop/core

http://www.eng.lsu.edu/mirrors/apache/hadoop/core

Select Stable

# Hadoop Releases

Please make sure you're downloading from a nearby mirror site, not from www.apac

We suggest downloading the current stable release.

Older releases are available from the archives.

| Name | Last modified | Size | Description |
|------|---------------|------|-------------|
| Parent Directory | | . | |
| current/ | 31-Mar-2014 05:19 | . | |
| current2/ | 31-Mar-2014 05:19 | . | |
| hadoop-0.23.10/ | 03-Dec-2013 01:07 | . | |
| hadoop-0.23.9/ | 01-Jul-2013 13:16 | . | |
| hadoop-1.2.1/ | 22-Jul-2013 18:49 | . | |
| hadoop-2.0.3-alpha/ | 06-Feb-2013 22:53 | . | |

## Select the tar.gz file ( not the file with src)

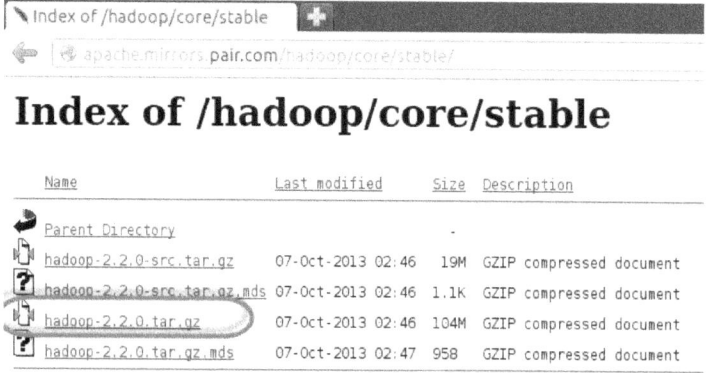

# Index of /hadoop/core/stable

| Name | Last modified | Size | Description |
|------|---------------|------|-------------|
| Parent Directory | | . | |
| hadoop-2.2.0-src.tar.gz | 07-Oct-2013 02:46 | 19M | GZIP compressed document |
| hadoop-2.2.0-src.tar.gz.mds | 07-Oct-2013 02:46 | 1.1K | GZIP compressed document |
| hadoop-2.2.0.tar.gz | 07-Oct-2013 02:46 | 104M | GZIP compressed document |
| hadoop-2.2.0.tar.gz.mds | 07-Oct-2013 02:47 | 958 | GZIP compressed document |

Once a download is complete, navigate to the directory containing the tar file

```
sbuser@ubuntu-virtualBox:~$ cd /home/ubuntu/Downloads
```

Enter,

```
sudo tar xzf hadoop-2.2.0.tar.gz
```

hduser_@guru99-VirtualBox:/home/guru99/Downloads$ sudo tar -xzf hadoop-2.2.0.tar.gz

## Now, rename hadoop-2.2.0 as hadoop

```
sudo mv hadoop-2.2.0 hadoop
```

hduser_@guru99-VirtualBox:/home/guru99/Downloads$ sudo mv hadoop-2.2.0 hadoop
hduser_@guru99-VirtualBox:/home/guru99/Downloads$

```
sudo chown -R hduser_:hadoop_ Hadoop
```

hduser_@guru99-VirtualBox:/home/guru99/Downloads$ sudo chown -R hduser_:hadoop_ hadoop
hduser_@guru99-VirtualBox:/home/guru99/Downloads$

# Part 2) Configure Hadoop

## Step 1) Modify ~/.bashrc file

Add following lines to end of file ~/.bashrc

```
#Set HADOOP_HOME
export HADOOP_HOME=<Installation Directory of
Hadoop>
#Set JAVA_HOME
export JAVA_HOME=<Installation Directory of
Java>
# Add bin/ directory of Hadoop to PATH
export PATH=$PATH:$HADOOP_HOME/bin
```

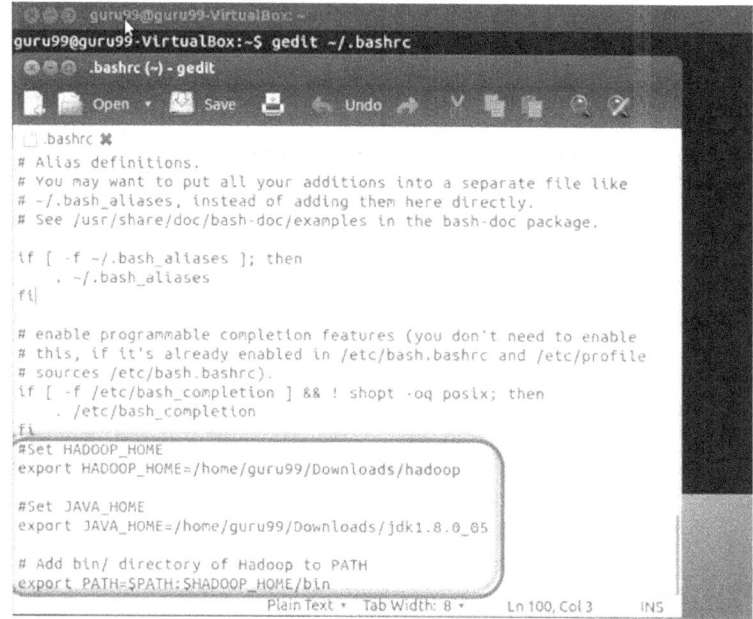

Now, source this environment configuration using below command

```
.  ~/.bashrc
```

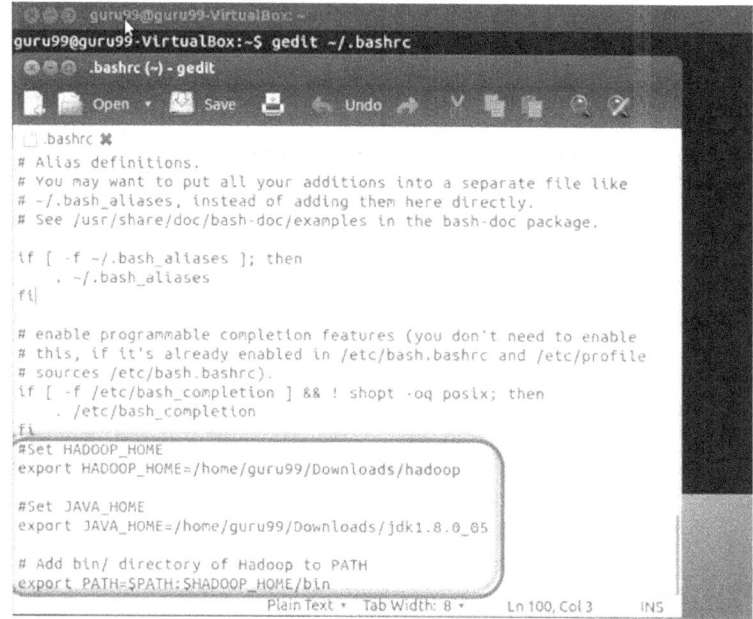

**Step 2)** Configurations related to HDFS

Set **JAVA_HOME** inside
file **$HADOOP_HOME/etc/hadoop/hadoop-env.sh**

```
guru99@guru99-VirtualBox:~$ sudo gedit /home/guru99/Downloads/hadoop/etc/hadoop/hadoop-env.sh
```

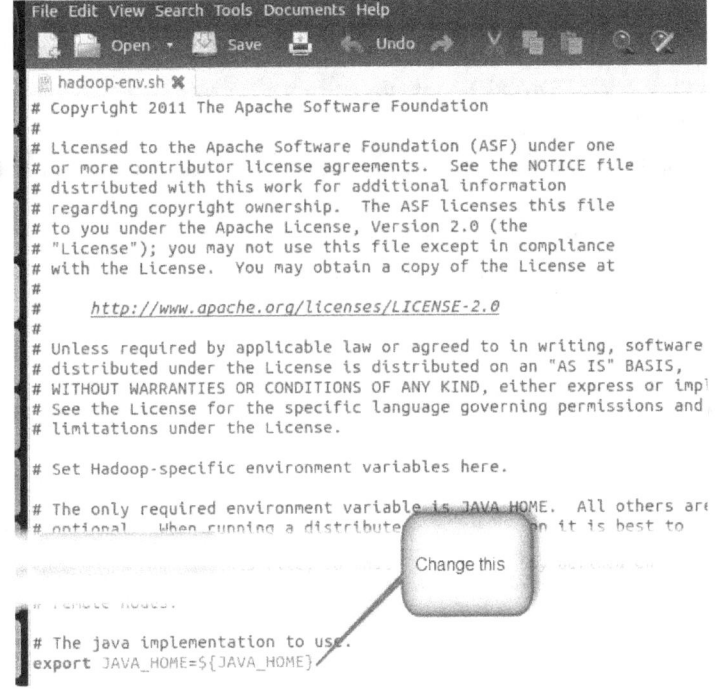

With

```
# The java implementation to use.
export JAVA_HOME=/home/guru99/Downloads/jdk1.8.0_05
```

There are two parameters in **$HADOOP_HOME/etc/hadoop/core-site.xml** which need to be set-

**1. 'hadoop.tmp.dir'** – Used to specify a directory which will be used by Hadoop to store its data files.

**2. 'fs.default.name'** – This specifies the default file system.

## To set these parameters, open core-site.xml

```
sudo gedit $HADOOP_HOME/etc/hadoop/core-
site.xml
```

әnιnәә@әnιnәә-ʌιιιnәιBox:~$ ᴢnqo ᴅᴇqιι \ʜoᴡᴇ\әnιnәә\ᴅoᴍᴜιoәqᴢ\ᴘәqoob\ᴇιc\ᴘәqoob\coιᴇ-ᴢιιᴇ·xᴡι

## Copy below line in between tags

```
<property>
<name>hadoop.tmp.dir</name>
<value>/app/hadoop/tmp</value>
<description>Parent directory for other
temporary directories.</description>
</property>
<property>
<name>fs.defaultFS </name>
<value>hdfs://localhost:54310</value>
<description>The name of the default file
system. </description>
</property>
```

```
core-site.xml (/usr/local/hadoop/etc/hadoop) - gedit
File Edit View Search Tools Documents Help
Open  •  Save     Undo

core-site.xml  ✕

        WITHOUT WARRANTIES OR CONDITIONS OF ANY KIND, either express or
implied.
    See the License for the specific language governing permissions and
    limitations under the License. See accompanying LICENSE file.
-->

<!-- Put site-specific property overrides in this file. -->

<configuration>
<property>
    <name>hadoop.tmp.dir</name>
    <value>/app/hadoop/tmp</value>
    <description>Parent directory for other temporary directories.</
description>
</property>

<property>
    <name>fs.defaultFS </name>
    <value>hdfs://localhost:54310</value>
    <description>The name of the default file system. </description>
</property>
</configuration>

                    XML  •   Tab Width: 8  •        Ln 22, Col 24       INS
```

Navigate to the
directory **$HADOOP_HOME/etc/Hadoop**

```
guru99@guru99-VirtualBox:~$ cd /home/guru99/Downloads/hadoop/etc/hadoop
guru99@guru99-VirtualBox:~/Downloads/hadoop/etc/hadoop$ 
```

Now, create the directory mentioned in core-site.xml

**sudo mkdir -p <Path of Directory used in above setting>**

```
guru99@guru99-VirtualBox:~/Downloads/hadoop/etc/hadoop$ sudo mkdir -p /app/hadoop/tmp
guru99@guru99-VirtualBox:~/Downloads/hadoop/etc/hadoop$ 
```

Grant permissions to the directory

sudo chown -R hduser_:Hadoop_ <Path of
Directory created in above step>

```
hduser_@guru99-VirtualBox:~$ sudo chown -R hduser_:hadoop_ /app/hadoop/tmp
hduser_@guru99-VirtualBox:~$ 
```

```
sudo chmod 750 <Path of Directory created in
above step>
```

```
hduser_@guru99-VirtualBox:~$ sudo chmod 750 /app/hadoop/tmp
hduser_@guru99-VirtualBox:~$
```

**Step 3)** Map Reduce Configuration

Before you begin with these configurations, lets set HADOOP_HOME path

```
sudo gedit /etc/profile.d/hadoop.sh
```
And Enter

```
export
HADOOP_HOME=/home/guru99/Downloads/Hadoop
```

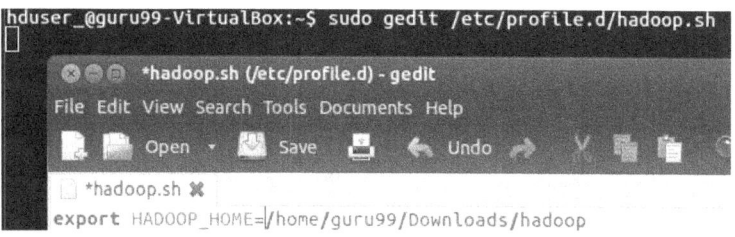

Next enter

```
sudo chmod +x /etc/profile.d/hadoop.sh
```

```
hduser_@guru99-VirtualBox:/$ sudo chmod +x /etc/profile.d/hadoop.sh
```

Exit the Terminal and restart again

Type echo $HADOOP_HOME. To verify the path

```
guru99@guru99-VirtualBox:~$ echo $HADOOP_HOME
/home/guru99/Downloads/hadoop
```

## Now copy files

```
sudo cp $HADOOP_HOME/etc/hadoop/mapred-
site.xml.template
$HADOOP_HOME/etc/hadoop/mapred-site.xml
```

```
late $HADOOP_HOME/etc/hadoop/mapred-site.xml
gurzaa@gurzaa-VirtualBox:~$ sudo cp $HADOOP_HOME/etc/hadoop/mapred-site.xml.temp
```

## Open the **mapred-site.xml** file

```
sudo gedit $HADOOP_HOME/etc/hadoop/mapred-
site.xml
```

```
gurzaa@gurzaa-VirtualBox:~$ sudo gedit $HADOOP_HOME/etc/hadoop/mapred-site.xml
```

## Add below lines of setting in between tags <configuration> and </configuration>

```
<property>
<name>mapreduce.jobtracker.address</name>
<value>localhost:54311</value>
<description>MapReduce job tracker runs at this
host and port.
</description>
</property>
```

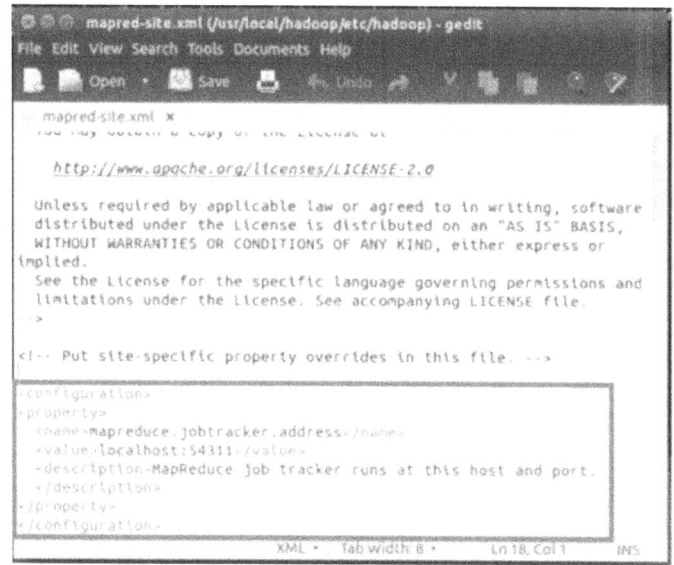

## Open $HADOOP_HOME/etc/hadoop/hdfs-site.xml as below,

```
sudo gedit $HADOOP_HOME/etc/hadoop/hdfs-site.xml
```

```
hduser_@guru99-VirtualBox:~$ sudo gedit $HADOOP_HOME/etc/hadoop/hdfs-site.xm
```

## Add below lines of setting between tags <configuration> and </configuration>

```
<property>
<name>dfs.replication</name>
<value>1</value>
<description>Default block
replication.</description>
</property>
<property>
<name>dfs.datanode.data.dir</name>
<value>/home/hduser_/hdfs</value>
```

```
</property>
```

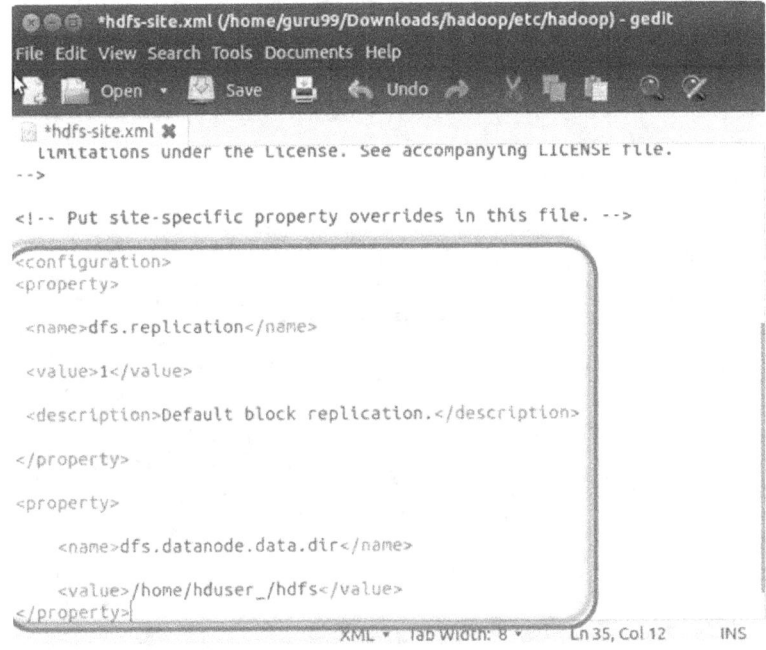

## Create a directory specified in above setting-

```
sudo mkdir -p <Path of Directory used in above
setting>
sudo mkdir -p /home/hduser_/hdfs
```

```
hduser_@guru99-VirtualBox:~$ sudo mkdir -p /home/hduser_/hdfs
```

```
sudo chown -R hduser_:hadoop_ <Path of
Directory created in above step>
sudo chown -R hduser_:hadoop_
/home/hduser_/hdfs
```

```
hduser_@guru99-VirtualBox:~$ sudo chown -R hduser_:hadoop_ /home/hduser_/hdfs
```

```
sudo chmod 750 <Path of Directory created in
above step>
```

```
sudo chmod 750 /home/hduser_/hdfs
```

```
hduser_@guru99-VirtualBox:~$ sudo chmod 750 /home/hduser_/hdfs
```

**Step 4)** Before we start Hadoop for the first time, format HDFS using below command

```
$HADOOP_HOME/bin/hdfs namenode -format
```

**Step 5)** Start Hadoop single node cluster using below command

```
$HADOOP_HOME/sbin/start-dfs.sh
```
An output of above command

```
$HADOOP_HOME/sbin/start-yarn.sh
```

```
hduser_@guru99-VirtualBox:~$ $HADOOP_HOME/sbin/start-yarn.sh
starting yarn daemons
starting resourcemanager, logging to /home/guru99/Downloads/hadoop/logs/yarn-hduser_-resourcemanager-guru9
9-VirtualBox.out
localhost: starting nodemanager, logging to /home/guru99/Downloads/hadoop/logs/yarn-hduser_-nodemanager-gu
ru99-VirtualBox.out
hduser_@guru99-VirtualBox:~$
```

Using **'jps'** tool/command, verify whether all the Hadoop related processes are running or not.

```
hduser_@guru99-VirtualBox:~$ jps
3732 SecondaryNameNode
4326 Jps
3865 ResourceManager
3466 DataNode
4061 NodeManager
3279 NameNode
hduser_@guru99-VirtualBox:~$
```

If Hadoop has started successfully then an output of jps should show NameNode, NodeManager, ResourceManager, SecondaryNameNode, DataNode.

**Step 6)** Stopping Hadoop

```
$HADOOP_HOME/sbin/stop-dfs.sh
```
```
hduser_@guru99-VirtualBox:~$ $HADOOP_HOME/sbin/stop-dfs.sh
Stopping namenodes on [localhost]
localhost: stopping namenode
localhost: stopping datanode
Stopping secondary namenodes [0.0.0.0]
0.0.0.0: stopping secondarynamenode
hduser_@guru99-VirtualBox:~$
```

**$HADOOP_HOME/sbin/stop-yarn.sh**

```
hduser_@guru99-VirtualBox:~$ $HADOOP_HOME/sbin/stop-yarn.sh
stopping yarn daemons
stopping resourcemanager
localhost: stopping nodemanager
no proxyserver to stop
hduser_@guru99-VirtualBox:~$
```

# Glossary

1. Big Data: Refers to large and complex datasets that are difficult to process and analyze using traditional data processing tools.

2. Data Analytics: The process of analyzing and interpreting data to gain insights and make data-driven decisions.

3. Data Science: An interdisciplinary field that involves using scientific methods, processes, algorithms, and systems to extract insights and knowledge from structured and unstructured data.

4. Data Warehouse: A centralized repository that stores structured data from multiple sources for reporting and analysis.

5. Data Lake: A centralized repository that stores raw, unstructured, and semi-structured data from multiple sources, making it easier for data

scientists and analysts to explore and analyze data.

6. Hadoop: An open-source distributed computing platform that enables the processing and storage of large datasets across clusters of computers.

7. MapReduce: A programming model and software framework for processing large datasets in parallel across multiple nodes in a Hadoop cluster.

8. Machine Learning: A branch of artificial intelligence that involves developing algorithms and statistical models that enable computers to learn from data and improve their performance on specific tasks over time.

9. Artificial Intelligence (AI): A broad field of computer science that involves developing intelligent systems that can perform tasks that typically require human intelligence, such as visual perception, speech recognition, and decision-making.

10. Internet of Things (IoT): The network of physical devices, vehicles, buildings, and other objects that are embedded with sensors, software, and network connectivity, enabling them to collect and exchange data.

11. Cloud Computing: The delivery of computing services, including servers, storage, databases, networking, software, analytics, and intelligence, over the internet ("the cloud").

12. Predictive Analytics: The use of statistical models and machine learning algorithms to analyze current and historical data to make predictions about future events.

13. Business Intelligence (BI): The use of data analytics tools and techniques to analyze and visualize data to support business decision-making.

14. Data Mining: The process of analyzing and discovering patterns and insights from large datasets using statistical and machine learning techniques.

15. NoSQL: A type of database that is designed to handle unstructured and semi-structured data and can scale horizontally across a cluster of commodity hardware.

www.ingramcontent.com/pod-product-compliance
Lightning Source LLC
Chambersburg PA
CBHW070510220526
45467CB00002B/612